SECRETS OF SPORTS BROADCASTING

PRACTICAL ADVICE FOR SPORTSCASTING SUCCESS

By Rick Schultz

More Sports Books by Rick Schultz on Amazon.com, iTunes and Audible.com - in Kindle, paperback and audio format:

Untold Tales from the Bush Leagues: A Behind the Scenes Look Into Minor League Baseball, From the Broadcasters Who Called the Action
More than 20 minor league baseball broadcasters share the most amazing, unbelievable and hilarious stories they have seen in the minor leagues. You will not believe what goes on in minor league baseball!

A Renegade Championship Summer: A Broadcaster's View of a Magical Minor League Baseball Season
Come along for the ride with the 1999 New York-Penn League Champion Hudson Valley Renegades. Hear from the players and coaches who made it happen, including superstar Josh Hamilton and many other household names! You'll get the true feel of minor league baseball, going behind the scenes with umpires, front office executives, scouts, former players and many more!

Minor League Baseball Revealed: A Secret Tour Inside Our National Pastime
Both books together in this compilation!

BONUS OFFER

As a special thanks for reading this book, please enjoy

HALF OFF OUR ONLINE SPORTS BROADCASTING COURSE

Visit Udemy.com/sportscasting

Use special code BOOKVIP

For my sports broadcasting friends and colleagues. It has been a pleasure to work with you over my 25 years in the crazy, exhilarating, challenging and demanding sports media industry.

And for my past, current and future students. These are many of the "secret" lessons I have learned along the way. May they help you along your road to success, and may they remain secret no longer!

Table of Contents

Preface

You really don't need me to figure out the secrets of sports broadcasting.

Honestly, you can do it all on your own.

It will only take you 25 years.

The biggest secret about the sports broadcasting industry is that there isn't just one secret, but rather a series of principles, philosophies and guidelines that can lead to success in the world of sports media. Anyone can acquire, attain and learn these secrets. For me, this took 25 years. And believe me, I'm not special. The learning continues to this day – from colleagues, students, mentors and everyone in between. One thing I learned a long time ago is that I can always be better.

We learn how to excel at the craft of sports broadcasting by starting with the advice of those who have gone before us, including many well-known pioneering media voices. We can take their wisdom to heart and make it our own. That is the quickest path to sports broadcasting achievement and most solid foundation for lasting success.

Over the last 25 years, I have been fortunate to learn from some of the biggest names in sportscasting. Some I have worked side by side with, in cramped broadcast booths or tight media quarters. Others have passed down their wisdom in classrooms, books, seminars or over the airwaves. They have done their best to demystify the industry, which is what I try to do every day for my online sports broadcasting students and those in the nationally-acclaimed sports department at WFUV Radio in New York City.

I believe the following tips and stories are the foundation on which to build a successful sports broadcasting career. And I can say as much without pretense because they don't belong to me. I didn't invent these philosophies and ideas, but rather I simply boiled them down over 25 years and use them to educate the next generation of sports broadcasting professionals. I hope you enjoy these stories and use them to create the best sports broadcasting career possible!

Please contact me at SportscastersClub.com and let me know what you think!

Baseball Broadcasting is Not What it Used to Be

I started my professional baseball broadcasting career in 1994. In many ways, that makes me feel like a broadcasting dinosaur. It is amazing to think back and recall how different baseball broadcasting is today, compared to two decades ago. I mean, honestly, I don't feel *that* old!

A baseball broadcaster's daily life has changed in many ways over the last twenty years.
Here are 10 important and surprising changes that jump to mind:

1. Riding minor league buses has never been fun, and never will be. Knees get sore and calves cramp just as they always did. However, 20 years ago, most players would pass time on long bus rides by playing cards or, if lucky, listening to a portable CD player. Occasionally you'd hit the jackpot and get to watch a good movie, if the bus had an overhead VCR and someone rented a VHS tape. (For those under 30, a VHS tape is one of those thin, rectangular boxes with spooled tape inside.)

I recall many long hours on the bus, reading the Book of Questions with former broadcast partner, Bill Rogan. We'd ask each other questions, such as "Would you rather stick your hand into a tub of snakes or a bee hive?" These conversations often got heated, and we passed the hours arguing and contemplating life's deep complexities.

Today, most everyone on the bus carries a portable computer, capable of instantaneous movies, videos, music, maps, conversation and communication. In other words, smart phones have phased out the Book of Questions. They contain any question, or answer, you could ever have.

2. In 1994 we did our pre and post-game interviews on cassette tapes. We would carefully record our interviews and then rewind and re-cue those tapes for play during the broadcast. If you were slick (which I sometimes was), you could make those interviews sound as if they were live. And we were actually fortunate, because we had just escaped the era of larger, reel-to-reel recording devices.

Today, most interviews are conducted with digital equipment, making recording and playback simple and efficient. You can basically do the entire process now with a cell phone and an internet connection.

3. During the 1998 home run chase between Mark McGwire and Sammy Sosa, we had fans constantly coming up to our radio booth, telling us when either of the two hit another home run. Fans would hear it on another radio broadcast and relay the information to us.

Today, you can watch, hear and read every moment of any sporting event in real time. The broadcaster truly has all the information at his fingertips in real time.

4. I had a few ways to supplement my income during the baseball season. After games, I would find a phone in the press box or in a vacant luxury suite, where I would call in the night's box score to a local newspaper. The paper would pay me $15 per game to call in and spend 15 minutes giving them all the details of the game, so they could print the recap the next morning.

Today, media can get much of this information digitally or online in real time. Struggling broadcasters have to find other ways to make a little extra dough.

5. In years gone by, media members would dine on free meals in press boxes before games. From a simple hot dog to more gourmet offerings, broadcasters always love a free meal.

Today, many professional ballclubs charge per-person for the pregame meal. The one bright spot is that the offerings are usually more appetizing than a simple dog and soda.

6. In the past, players' families would often listen in to games on radio networks or, on occasion, on newly-formed internet broadcasting stations. If a broadcaster was critical of a player, that player's family would hear it and let the player know the next time they talked by phone. By the time what you said got back to the player, his version was usually much worse than what you *actually* had said. Nothing like the good, old-fashioned telephone game to get a player, or many, annoyed with you.

Today, everything is done in real time. Fans, family and even players can listen live and get the true version of what you say, as you say it. Pitchers in the bullpen will often listen to game broadcasts, and used to wave their hats to me when I said something they liked. If I chose to rip on them, they'd show their disgust by kicking up a storm of dirt. As long as you are fair, you'd always rather have an athlete hear your comments first hand.

7. Minor league baseball is a traveling freak show circus. With a game every night, from town to town, the life can be quite crazy. Players, and the media, have been known to partake in their share of late-night shenanigans.

Today.....ok so not everything has changed.

8. Broadcasters in the 90's had to proactively market themselves to prospective employers through bulky, mailed packages, containing demo cassette tapes, physical resumes, press clippings and other materials.

Today, much of the career networking and resume sharing can be done electronically. You can never replace the human touch that helps you stand out, however today's technology offers immense time-saving advantages.

9. Radio play by play guys were always headed on a long trip. At least that was the way it looked, as they lugged huge, overloaded suitcases containing their radio broadcasting equipment. It was a workout dragging that 100 pound tub from the press box to the team bus, along with personal bags and belongings.

Today, equipment is much more compact and lightweight. Some say that makes today's broadcasters soft compared to the tough guys around a couple decades ago. I'd say they are more efficient.

10. Years ago, some broadcasters would chronicle their games and travels into diaries, journals and books.

Today, they simple log on and bang out a post on a super-cool, hugely-followed sports broadcasting blog. Or better yet, they give up-to-the-moment updates on Twitter and Facebook.

One thing is for sure – modern technology has increased the speed and efficiency of our communication, and brought sports broadcasters and fans closer than ever to the action. I can only imagine what the next 20 years will bring!

Sacrifice for Your Sportscasting Dream

A while back, a broadcaster dropped me a tweet, wanting to get into baseball broadcasting. His question was simple. "How do I get started?"

I subsequently posted some effective steps for new broadcasters to break into the industry.

As a follow up, here is just a quick point about sacrifice. The sacrifice you'll need to make to break into the broadcasting business. For many, it includes working for free. And working holidays, and birthdays, and inconvenient times when your friends are out partying like normal 20-somethings. If you want to work on air, or in media, you must choose to build your career rather than enhancing your social life. Not all the time, but often enough.

In 1994 I received a phone call on Christmas morning. A friend at NBC TV in Manhattan needed a warm body to help log tape in the NBC Sports studios that night from 5pm to midnight. Although I didn't know anything about "logging tape," I quickly cancelled my Christmas plans and hopped a train down to NYC to work my first of what turned out to be years of shifts at NBC. These shifts logging details of every NFL or College Football play eventually led to a regular weekend schedule of games at NBC, followed later by work at ABC Sports as well.

The Christmas sacrifice I made many years ago led to future opportunities and helped me build many key relationships. To be in the broadcasting business, you may have to make your own similar sacrifices as well.

Will You Be a Sportscasting Failure?

There is a sure-fire way to fail at sports broadcasting. Not a specific technique or lack of skill that will cause your demise, but rather an overall *approach*. Learn this lesson, and learn what *not* to do.

Nearly 20 years ago, while broadcasting minor league baseball, I encountered two truly great guys. This duo was the broadcast team for a division rival, which meant we caught up with each other a dozen times per season.

The two broadcasters shared the same name - Joe. (No, not their real name) However, they were so different that we gave them each a nickname. One was Professional Joe and the other was Unprofessional Joe. Here's why.

Professional Joe would show up to the ballpark hours before the game, diligently preparing himself for the broadcast. This guy knew what it took to succeed in sports broadcasting. Unprofessional Joe, meanwhile, would strut in casually shortly before first pitch.

Professional Joe dressed the part - cleanly shaved in neat pants and a collared shirt. Unprofessional Joe usually hadn't touched a razor in days, and was usually decked out in shorts and a t-shirt.

Professional Joe would invest time near the dugout and batting cage before the game, curiously asking players questions and gathering valuable information to spice up his broadcast. Unprofessional Joe used to hang out in the dugout before the game too - literally, he used to hang from the top of the dugout and practice quasi-gymnastic moves to draw a laugh.

Both Professional Joe and Unprofessional Joe were terrific guys, the kind you'd enjoy spending an evening at the ballpark with. Their overall approach, however, was what separated these two friends and broadcast partners.

Unprofessional Joe wasn't part of the team's broadcast crew the following season. Unprofessional sports broadcasters usually don't stick around very long.

Absolutely Amazing!

I cringe every time I hear a broadcaster speak in absolute terms. Because one thing is for sure – things can *absolutely* change.

What do I mean?

How often do you hear a sportscaster say something like:

"That was the most amazing catch I've ever seen!"
"This is the best team ever!"
"They will never come back from this deficit."
"That is the most ridiculous thing I've ever seen."

When using words and phrases that are so absolute in nature, you leave yourself no wiggle room. You need some room to adapt and adjust. The "most amazing catch you've ever seen." Perhaps 20 years ago you saw one even more magnificent, even if you can't recall it off the top of your head. Use caution when speaking in these absolute terms. At times they may be appropriate. More often than not, they aren't.

As a broadcaster, language has meaning. Take care when using words such as most, best, worst, never, etc. In the dynamic world of sportscasting, things change. Often. Always.

That much is absolutely true.

Are Sportscasters Really Independent?

Each year as I celebrate America's Independence Day, I chew on this question with my burgers and dogs. Are Sportscasters are really independent? In other words, can they speak their mind as a journalist without repercussion? The no-fluff answer - yes and no.

Sportscasting gigs are as varied as can be. In some positions, the broadcaster is given free reign. In others, he is closely monitored and controlled. I've worked on both ends of the spectrum and students would often ask me about what they should expect.

I called games for one minor league team for six seasons, and not once did any member of the front office ever confront me for something I said on the air. (Players, employees and fans sure did, but never did a person of real power try to cramp my style.) The team allowed me to be honest, truthful and open with my audience, as I shared facts and, occasionally, opinion.

I also broadcast for a Double-A ballclub, and the General Manager pulled me aside and tried to curtail my on-air speech the very first week of the season. I had begun the ballgame by telling listeners it was 37 degrees on that frigid April evening. I painted the word picture, detailing the intrepid fans bundled up for warmth in the brutal conditions. The General Manager popped into the booth and told me my honesty would keep fans away from the park if I persisted. He told me to cut it out. I argued that my listeners were much smarter than that and weren't going to stay home based on something I said about what they can feel for themselves. While I understood his point as someone running a business, I wasn't a cheerleader. I was a journalist, and journalists report.

When I did play by play for Army basketball and hockey at West Point, I heard all the talk about how controlling and tightly-wound the Army brass was toward its public relations and broadcasting. However, they never curtailed me a bit, and I always appreciated the freedom to do my job. Perhaps my professional, buttoned-up style was a great fit, or maybe they never listened. Either way, calling Army games at West Point was a terrific time in my career.

The point is, some broadcasters have more leeway to speak freely and be themselves. And to a degree, it has to do with what medium or position you are working in. A talk-show host may have different constraints than a play-by-play man. Ultimately however, station management will be the key. You may have to work for some real pains in this industry, but eventually you can find the match that best suits your personality.

I wish you a wonderful career as a thoughtful, independent sportscaster!

Ballplayer Envy

It's that time of year again. No, I'm not talking about turkey and Christmas trees. Each off-season, you can count on hearing the cries from baseball fans far and wide, crying foul over another huge, multi-million dollar baseball contract. We all do it at times. In some ways its part of being a fan.

With every new, astronomical signing, I ask - why demonize the players for earning every dime they can get? Wouldn't you?

Many years ago, I sat with an athlete after he received a signing bonus worth over $10 million.
"The point of a huge bonus," his mother said, "is that now he can simply concentrate on baseball. The money will take care of all the necessary pitfalls of everyday life, and he can keep himself focused 100 percent on being the best ballplayer he can be."

Beyond that, however, it is simply a matter of supply and demand. There are a limited number of premier athletes with skills that consumers are willing to pay big bucks to see. Period. Regardless of the sport, these are the top fraction of a percent of all who play the game. And we, as fans, have always been willing to pay.

I just wish we'd hear less of the envious, negative opinions when talking about a player's new free-agent deal. Am I wrong to admire a great talent for earning every penny he is worth in the marketplace?

Broadcasters crashing to the floor

We stayed in a hotel recently. When I went to grab the iron out of the closet, the entire bracket came crashing down off the wall. It appeared to have been put up hastily, and without the parts necessary to keep it secure. Soon after, I began seeing other things around the suite that we just not up to par. Now I was looking, and I was finding a lot I didn't like. One mistake had keyed me in and led me to look for – and find – others.

As a broadcaster, we must keep this scenario in mind. Our most valued quality is our broadcast integrity. Fooling listeners with incorrect facts or guesses can only lead to one thing – a loss of trust in you, the broadcaster. If you are caught in incorrect statements, listeners immediately begin to question everything you say. If you are wrong or misleading once, who's to say you won't do it again and again.

Sportscasters cannot know everything there is to know about a particular event, team or player. A top national sportscaster gave me great advice back in 1994, when I was just getting into sports broadcasting.

"If you don't know, don't be afraid to admit it. Don't ever fake it."

Once a broadcaster is caught faking it, it takes an awful long time to regain the listener's trust, if it can be done at all.

The next time you don't have the answer on air, just say so. Or just go find the answer. Either way, don't become the iron that crashes to the floor.

Broadcasting Because Of Dad

Each Father's Day, I'm reminded of a question I've gotten quite often from broadcast students.

"Do some broadcasters get their job just because of who their Dad is?"

The answer is very simple - yes.

There are plenty of examples of media professionals who hold positions solely because their Dad was a big time broadcaster, executive or power player of some sort. It's true, get used to it. And the truth is that some of them are just not good enough to get there on their own. I've always felt that out of...let's say 150 minor league baseball broadcasters, there are at least a couple dozen that are skilled enough and should be in the big leagues.
The cynical trap many fall into, however, is to think broadcasting is any different than any other area of life.

Do some business professionals rise to their rank only because of their genealogy? Of course. Are some entertainers riding high because of big daddy's pockets? Certainly. It also happens to managers, accountants, attorneys and janitors too. That's life.

Because broadcasters are in the public eye, it seems that so many of them are simply picked because of who their father was. The truth, however, is that it's probably the same percentage as in any other area of life. In addition, for each one who may be undeserving, there's a Joe Buck who has risen to become a legit number one, regardless of his bloodlines. In fact, give him credit for learning from a master, his Dad Jack Buck. He overcame the double-edged sword of having to grow through his father's shadow.

As a broadcaster, don't let yourself become too jaded to see that YOU control YOU. Life isn't always fair, and this industry is no different. You can't worry about other people from other situations. Life is too short. You've got a game to do.

Networking for Broadcasters

"Teenagers these days don't hang out with each other. Instead, they stay home on the couch and talk through their phones."

A mother recently told me this about her teenage daughter. Aside from being quite scary, this also gives us a great insight into the psyche of the younger generation of professionals, including sports broadcasters.

Technology is a terrific way to create, build and expand your brand as a broadcast professional. Sports broadcasters are able to network and share like never before. This is not just a good thing, but a GREAT thing for building your broadcasting career!

Don't think for a moment, however, that you can lay at home on the couch and "virtually" network your way to the sports broadcasting career of your dreams. For this, you'll still need good old-fashioned people skills. You know, those communications abilities you paid the school tens of thousands for. Just ask our friend, Dan Miller. His advice for landing that dream job is priceless.

New technological advances are wonderful for building and growing your sportscasting business, but don't be fooled into believing this alone is enough. You still must get out there and make it happen. And that means flipping off the phone and getting out into the world with real people.

Broadcasting Regardless

We heard a sportscaster the other day, rambling on about how a player did something "irregardless" of the situation. Sharp listeners probably cringe when they hear that word. And boy do we hear it often.

Most dictionaries, such as Merriam-Webster, are clear that the correct word would simply be "regardless." While they agree there is, indeed, such a word...it is nonstandard. If that weren't enough, try using the word in any basic Word document. You'll get the squiggly, red line underneath - showing that it is a spelling error!

If Webster says it's nonstandard, broadcasters should do better. Most who use it are just lazy. Some don't know this word really isn't a proper word.

Sportscasters should be proper and precise. Viewers and listeners deserve it, irregardless.

Bus Ride Mania

A few years ago, a minor league baseball team was involved in a relatively minor accident, as their bus hit a truck and a guardrail during an overnight trip. As I read some of the tweets from the players, and it brought back some crazy minor league memories.

I was once on a bus with a team as we departed for a long, daytime trip. Not even a mile from the park, we watch a tractor trailer collide with another vehicle right in front of us. The driver was knocked unconscious.

I also recall the middle-of-the-night wakeup when our bus just missed being slammed by a passing train at a railroad crossing. Or the time the axles on the left side of the bus busted and we cruised into town with the bus tilted to the left. We looked like a circus act coming to town. The bus was tilted about a foot, and the driver later told me we could have tipped over quite easily.

I've heard of players finding snakes next to their bus, and seen players sleep inside the small, overhead compartments. I've seen fistfights onboard, as well as bleary-eyed, beer-filled celebrations. Stay in this game long enough and you'll see just about anything on that bus.

How glamorous it is.

Keep Your Shirt On

Minor league baseball life is not glamorous at all. At least most of the time. As a result, minor league broadcasters often find humor in the smallest things. You are in a season-long bubble and trivial events can seem SOOO important. It's as if you become numb to the real world after living inside the daily, minor league cocoon.

One example of this worldwide phenomenon is the story involving a minor league baseball pitcher. He and his team were riding the bus in the Bush Leagues one night after the game, when the bus stopped to allow the players to grab "dinner" in the convenience store.

After about 30 minutes, most of the players were safely back in their seats on the bus, ready for the long trip ahead. All the players except for one.

A few minutes later the door to the convenience store popped open and out darted a stray cat, which scampered across the street and into the darkness. A moment later, the pitcher slowly ambled out and up into the bus. The right sleeve of his multi-colored, silk summer shirt was ripped and nearly torn from his torso. He looked as if he'd been involved in a bar fight, and the team erupted in laughter upon seeing him enter the bus.

"I found this cat in the store," he explained "I tried to rescue it and get it home safely, but while I was cornering the cat near the chips I caught my shirt on the rack and ripped this huge hole!"

Although a bit sore, the pitcher was back on the mound the next day. Even more ridiculous than that....inside the Groundhog Day of minor league baseball, this was a big deal to us. We joked about it for days. Such is the glamorous life of minor league baseball.

Does Your Mother Do This?

While watching the great Al Michaels call a football game recently, I recalled some wisdom I learned almost 20 years ago from broadcasting legend Marty Glickman. At Fordham, Marty would talk sportscasting for hours. Listening to our tapes and letting us have it – no sugar-coating, just the good and bad. I consider his sage sportscasting advice often and, while listening to Michaels, I reflected on one of his most unambiguous points.

Al Michaels is a terrific play by play announcer in my opinion. Smooth, abundantly prepared and quick on his feet. Michaels has been a mainstay on the national football scene for decades, calling some of the biggest games in NFL history. I am always pleased when I tune in to a game and find Michaels behind the microphone, and I think aspiring sportscasters should take note.

One main thought Marty Glickman constantly drove home - to which Michaels clearly adheres - is that nobody tunes in to hear a broadcaster. We all tune in *for the game*, not the broadcaster, regardless of how wonderful we think they are. Solid broadcasters certainly add to the action, while lousy ones can detract from it. However, we tune in for the game itself. In fact the way Marty put it, "The only person who tunes in to hear the broadcaster is his mother!"

As play by play broadcasters, this should constantly put our ultimate duties – to inform, enlighten and entertain - in perspective. We should be facilitating the fans' enjoyment of the game, not trying to become a major part of it. I understand I may have some disagreement around Bristol, Connecticut or some other media outlets that push "attitude" above all else. Sorry, but I agree with Marty Glickman.

And so I leave you with this question. Is there any time you tune in to a game to hear the broadcaster?

Amateur or Professional Sportscaster?

Amateur broadcasters think people tune in to hear them on the air.
Professional broadcasters know fans tune in for *the game*.

Amateur broadcasters think talent is the most important ingredient to their success.
Professional broadcasters know talent is nothing without passion and hard work.

Amateur broadcasters think sports broadcasting leads to a glamorous life.
Professional sportscasters know that there is no guarantee of a glamorous life.

Amateur sports broadcasters expect to hit the big time shortly after graduating college.
Professional sportscasters are prepared to work for little or no money during, or even after, college.

Amateur sportscasters think they know it all.
Professional sports broadcasters know they will *never* know it all.

Amateur broadcasters think the big-timers won't help them.
Professional broadcasters help others because they were once helped.

Amateur sportscasters show up to work hard on the air.
Professional sportscasters work hard and *then* show up to broadcast.

Amateur sports broadcasters clock in and out with complacency.
Professional sports broadcasters are always reading, learning and improving.

Which are you?

Don't I Feel Stupid

Boy, did I feel like a jerk on one particular day at the ballpark in the mid-90's. (Not that it hasn't happened a few times since)

I was sitting in the broadcast booth, diligently preparing my pre-game notes and scorebook for that night's game. It was just 3:00 pm, and I had plenty of work to do on this simmering-hot, summer day.
"Hey Rick," my broadcast partner Bill Rogan called, as he entered the booth. "There are some people I'd like you to meet today. A young boy, Tommy, is coming by today to shadow you for a school project. He's a really big fan of yours. He'd like to know what it takes to become a sportscaster, and he has a lot of questions. He's going to be looking for you around 4:00. He is really looking forward to meeting you. Is that ok?"

I felt honored. Sure I'd share some of my time, especially if I can help make a difference for a young, aspiring broadcaster! If he was coming especially to pick my brain, I was ready to give him all the information he'd want.

About an hour later, as I sat working alone in the booth, a young boy and his mother approached my window.
"Oh, you must be Tommy," I said as I bounded out of the booth wearing a big, eager smile. "I'm Rick Schultz, great to meet you! Come on in, let me show you around the park while we talk."

For the next hour I gave young Tommy the lowdown on the baseball broadcasting business. I went through my pre-game duties, explaining each step to him in detail. He looked on, only with mild interest.

Since Tommy and his mother were at the park that day specifically to see me, I spent a lot of the afternoon detailing my background, my experience and how I'd become a professional broadcaster at the young age of 18. I was pumped to share my story, although they seemed distracted and somewhat disinterested.

After a while, Tommy and his mother politely thanked me and said they had to run. With that, they backed away and quickly left the park. I was a bit surprised at how quickly they seemed to leave, but I put my confusion aside and went back to my pre-game work.

As game time approached, Bill returned and we resumed preparations for that night's game. Just then our boss from the radio station popped in.
"Hey guys, how's it going?" he asked. "How did it go with that young student today? He was really looking forward to meeting you Bill."

I whipped my head around and asked, incredulously, "Did you say he was here to see BILL?"

"Of course," the boss said. "We set it up in advance, he's a big fan of Bill's."

At that moment - it hit me. I had introduced myself to a boy and his mother and told them all about myself and my career. I had detailed what I do and how I do it. I had offered my best advice and guidance to this young boy and his mother. And, as it turns out, they weren't even there to see me! While I thought they were *my* fans, in reality they probably didn't have any idea at all who I was!

To steal a quote from "A Few Good Men"......don't I feel like a...big, self-centered jerk.

(Don't worry, though, because I did get Bill back. Ask him about the ice in his hotel room bed.)

Help Me See the Game

Play by play broadcasters know it's all about the eyes.
On radio, your main focus should be your *listener's* eyes.

Radio voices know their primary duty is to paint the word
picture and let the listener "see" the game. Let your words
give them vision. Radio sportscasters give vision by
painting that word picture in the mind's eye of the listener.

A broadcast colleague once told me of the blind season-
ticket holder, who would sit aside him and "watch" the
game. He saw and felt the action through the broadcaster's
words. Descriptive terminology. Precise court
geography. An active vocabulary. These all played their
part in the blind fan being able to see the game.

I've always kept this fan in my mind when calling a game.
He made me a much more detailed and accurate
sportscaster.

Do you think he can help you too?

Cooperstown

The Baseball Hall of Fame in Cooperstown, New York is a special place. A magical place. If you've never been, put it on your list. I guarantee you'll have memories that will last a lifetime.

The first time I visited the mystical town in central New York was during a frigid March in the early 1990's, when my father and I camped out on the front steps of the Hall of Fame to get tickets for that year's Hall of Fame game.

Tickets were hard to come by, and we were second in line right in front of the main doors to the Hall. We had sleeping bags, folding chairs, coats and blankets to brave the temperatures in the teens. We took turns sitting in the heated car parked up the street, and I also recall an extremely drunken local named Doodles. He came wandering down near the line of fans and was soon arrested for public intoxication. A while later, in the middle of the brutally cold night, a few of his drunken friends came by and began chanting, "Free Doodles! Free Doodles!" This was my first memory of Baseball's Hall of Fame.

The next morning, after purchasing our tickets, we took a casual stroll through the Hall of Fame. On this March day, the Hall was virtually empty and it seemed like a private tour.

I have returned to Cooperstown a handful of times since that day, first as a fan and then as a broadcaster. While in high school, I corralled a couple friends and drove up during Reggie Jackson's induction weekend. I walked the back alleys, gathering (and paying for) autographs from some of the game's greats – Enos Slaughter, Warren Spahn, etc. I didn't have much cash, but I spent it all on autographs, trinkets and baseball knickknacks.

In 1994, I joined the Hudson Valley Renegades for the team's day trip to Cooperstown while playing a night game in nearby Oneonta.

"Are you coming with us to the Hall of Fame?" team manager Doug Sisson asked me that morning.

"If I can," I replied. I was an 18 year old, unpaid broadcaster helping out the team's full-time voice.

"Of course you can," he said defiantly. "You're part of this team!"

That day I stood in the Hall watching Reid Ryan, who was observing a throng of fans who were marveling at a display honoring his father, Nolan. Stephen Larkin, Barry's younger brother, was also touring the Hall with us that day. As was current Miami Marlins General Manager, Michael Hill, then a player.

A few years later, I returned to the Hall of Fame with another Renegades team, and had a chance to see yet another set of displays. I had a picture taken with Greg Harris, in front of a glass case holding his glove. In 1995 he had become the only pitcher in baseball history to throw with both arms in the same inning. The glove displayed at the Hall of Fame could fit either hand.

I made the trip back to Cooperstown in 1999, this time as the Renegades broadcaster. During my pregame interview before the Renegades contest at Doubleday Field, I asked hitting coach Jose Ortiz if he had ever been in the Hall of Fame.

"Well, I guess I'm in there somehow," he said. "After being around the game so long, I'm sure I have some connection."

"No," I responded. "I meant have you ever actually been inside and walked around." Yes, he had.

After the Renegades won that game, I sat across the street with one of the team's pitchers, reminiscing about Cooperstown and the remarkable Hall of Fame. The place has been the source of so many terrific memories for so many baseball fans. As you watch this year's induction ceremonies, I hope you are making plans to visit Cooperstown as well. As a matter of fact, I think I need to do it again sometime soon.

I Need My Big Broadcasting Break

You've probably heard that phrase a few times, especially if you are in the media or sports broadcasting business.

I recently received an email from a despondent broadcast professional who was wondering when he'd get his big break. My advice to him was that he would eventually get his big break, provided he was willing to struggle, sacrifice and push through until that day arrived.

Some get the big break sooner than later. Some broadcasters simply get to a point where the dream doesn't justify the sacrifice. A great majority of broadcasters tailor their "dream" to create their own breaks and make it fit into their new career framework.

Broadcasters understand exactly what I mean. For most sportscasters, the days are usually long and hard before one reaches higher levels of success.

For this reason, you need to determine the true "WHY" behind your career aspirations. Once you do, you need some kind of roadmap to keep you on target to reach your full potential. Only with the "WHY" in full view can you make the necessary daily sacrifices to build your dream.

What is your "WHY?"

The Worst Host in the World

Saw a tweet recently that reminded me of a sage piece of broadcasting wisdom.

The tweet simply read, "Knicks hosting Bucks."

I was reminded of my days at Fordham University, during one of our Tuesday sportscasting sessions with legendary broadcast coach Marty Glickman.

If the Knicks are "hosting" the Bucks, are they laying out a decadent spread of tea and crumpets? Serving wine and cheese? An Italian feast? Are they meeting the Bucks at the curb and hauling their luggage into MSG? Putting them up in the guest room with a fresh set of linens and towels?

Now that's a host!

Marty was a stickler for the language. He wanted broadcasters to be genuine and precise.

The choice is up to you. You can be run-of-the-mill, or you can be unique. Are you satisfied being just another face in the crowd, saying the Knicks are "hosting" the Bucks? Or will you stand out by being different?

Broadcasting a Dog

Sometimes the game just plain stinks! There's nothing you can do. You prepare, you plan, and you prepare some more.....and then when the lights go on, the game is an absolute DOG!

As a broadcaster, a main focus of our job should be to prepare as though the game will be a blowout. Most competent voices can call a close nail-biter, but it's the real pro's pro that can make a yawner seem important or, dare I say, exciting.

The broadcaster should never become the main attraction, however in a blowout a little levity can go a long way. This is when personality and the value you bring from thorough preparation carries the day.

Think about that next time you prepare to broadcast a dog of a game.

Woof Woof!

How to Get a Start in Sports Broadcasting

"Where do I start?"

That is the question I get most often from aspiring sportscasters, especially those in high school or college. I spent hours answering that question each week while teaching at Marist College and the Connecticut School of Broadcasting, and I now discuss it often with my team at Fordham University. I also get emails and tweets periodically, asking me how to begin a sportscasting career.

The truth is, there are many ways to get a start in broadcasting. First, understand that this is a tough industry, filled with excitement and pitfalls. I've always given students the unvarnished truth.
This is not a complete list of how-to's for beginning a career, but merely a quick group of bullet points. We could devote hours to each one. Hopefully these act as a quick jumping-off point to get you headed in the right way.

1. Practice – Commit to daily improvement. Broadcast games. Increase your knowledge. Become a better broadcaster every day.

2. Do It For Free – Often you must work for free to gain experience and prove your value in the media

marketplace. Use these opportunities to the fullest, as they will provide your launching pad to greater, paying opportunities!

3. Find a mentor, or ten – Most established sportscasting professionals are willing to help. Use them! Ask questions!

4. Leverage your contacts – Whether from your college, high school or community, make the most of your contact network. Let them know who you are and what your goals are.

5. Read – Perhaps the most important step of all. Read everything, to sharpen your philosophies, likes and dislikes. Read the history of what you want to be involved in. Know the games, traditions and rules.

6. Use technology as one tool in your bag – The internet is great, but not everything. I can post wonderful information on Twitter, Facebook, YouTube, etc., but eventually it comes down to being a real person.

7. Remain hungry – Sportscasting will challenge your will. Decide what your goals are and constantly strive to reach them.

I got started in this business by selling programs at the ballpark and becoming friendly with team's radiocaster. I also did 5:00 am newscasts every day before college classes....for free. Do you think I enjoyed getting up that early every morning? No, but you can bet that almost 25 years later I am glad I did.

How do you plan to start your sports broadcasting career? As a special thanks for reading this book, please enjoy half off our online sports broadcasting course.
Simply visit Udemy.com/sportscasting and use the special, top-secret promo code BOOKVIP

Is It Really About You?

Why do so many broadcasters make it all about them?

During a recent NFL broadcast, they threw it down to the sideline reporter as the second half was about to begin. She started, "Well I just talked with Coach Jim Harbaugh, who told me….blah blah blah…"

Why is it about her? Why not just say, "Coach Jim Harbaugh just said…."

Fans are watching to see the game and hear about its participants.
Of course you talked to him, but we don't care. After all, it's your job.
Some broadcasters just like you to know that they were just talking to an NFL coach.

Many broadcasters simply fall into the lazy habits of the pack.

Successful, secure sportscasters try to cut to the chase and leave themselves out of it.

Keep Your Focus on the Field

I received a tweet yesterday that I disagreed with completely.

The author was thrilled that a football television broadcast included so many great crowd shots during the exciting game. Philosophically, I couldn't disagree more.

A broadcaster's role is, in a sense, to put the viewer in the seat next to you at the game. What can I do to make the viewer feel as though he is sitting in the arena? How can I make them feel as if they are at the game?

I've been to many an exciting game in my day, both as a fan and as a broadcaster. I can honestly say that – with the exception of an occasional high-five and casual conversation – I hardly ever scan the crowd looking to see how other fans are reacting. Since I'm at the game, I'm watching *the game*. That's precisely why I'm there! I'm not wasting my time watching how fans are reacting to the game that I paid to watch myself.

That's not to say an occasionally crowd shot – during down time – shouldn't be a value added to the telecast. But only sporadically, and certainly not where they become intrusive.

Next time you're at a game, look around. Are fans constantly turning their heads, gazing into the crowd, rather than onto the field? Nope, they are watching the game. That is why they are there! The telecast should reflect the occasional glance, rather than the over-used shots of crazed fanatics.

Your job as a broadcaster is to bring the viewer as close as possible to the action. That is the goal of your television broadcast.

Am I wrong?

The Great Ralph Kiner

Ralph Kiner was everything that makes baseball special. From his slugging career to his grandfatherly commentary, Ralph Kiner made you feel connected to the game.

Much has been written about Kiner since his passing in 2014. A lengthy tribute so well deserved.

One of his most well-known broadcasting insights was that "Two thirds of the earth is covered by water; the rest is covered by Garry Maddox."

Kiner always gave the viewer an honest answer, sprinkled with anecdotes and experiences. When asked why he didn't choke up on the bat, Kiner said, in his ever-honest style, "Cadillacs are down at the end of the bat."

For so many fans and broadcasters, Kiner was a connection to baseball's glorious past. Thankfully, his impact still endures in New York, Pittsburgh and across the baseball world.

Watch Out for the Lazy Sportscaster

How can you tell the lazy sports broadcasters?
Just count the clichés and crutch phrases.

Sports broadcasting is no different than any form of communication - be as clear and concise as you can to increase the precision with which your message resonates. Simple, right?

So why, then, do sports fans constantly hear their favorite broadcasters spewing nonstop cliché and crutch words?

Some examples....

"He's just *not on the same page* with his catcher."
Are they in a book club together?

"Tonight they need to give *110%*"
Is there such a thing?

"They really *stepped it up* in *crunch time*"
Up to where? Is it Nestle Crunch?

"Jones on the right, passes *now* to Davis left baseline"
When else would it be?

"We've got a great game *here* tonight"
Where else would it be?

"Now we send it down to Joe with our player of the game"
"*Thanks Dave,* I'm here with....."
What are you thanking him for?

"Well, this team just *didn't show up* tonight"
Really? Was it a forfeit?

"*Defense wins championships*"
 Not if the other team plays slightly better defense.

"The game is *on the line*"
The clothes line?

OK, you get the picture. Much of what we sports fans and broadcasters actually say during and about our favorite sport is complete nonsense.

What are your favorite - or least favorite - sports clichés?

Proper English on the Hardcourt

Isn't it great when we hear the English language used properly?

During the NBA's Eastern Conference Finals a few years ago, Celtics point guard Rajon Rondo took aim at his opponent, the Miami Heat, saying the Heat were complaining too much about the referees.

When asked about those comments after Game 4 of the series, Heat Coach Erik Spoelstra said, "I could really care less..." However he quickly changed the beginning of his statement to, "I *couldn't* care less...." Bravo coach!

When he started by saying he "could" care less, that implies he actually cares a little. By changing it to "couldn't" care less, it means he is already at the lowest level of caring.

Am I the only one who still applauds when the language is used correctly? Am I the only one so....ahem...uptight about such things?

How many broadcasters could pass this high standard?

Would you?

Saying nothing on the air

Way back in 2012, during Mets pitcher Johan Santana's remarkable no-hitter, I saw a terrific broadcaster do a terrific job by saying nothing. Hugh? But isn't a broadcaster supposed to talk? And most DO! They talk, and talk and talk. And more than a few yell and yell and yell. So how can a broadcaster succeed by saying nothing? The goal of the play by play broadcaster is to bring the listener into the game, so to speak. The great Marty Glickman used to say he wanted the viewer/listener to "feel" as if they were sitting next to him at the game. Let them experience every emotion along with each fan in the stands.

On the final pitch of the no-no, Mets TV play by play man Gary Cohen exuberantly declared that Santana had completed the first no-hitter in Mets history…..and then he shut up! For 64 seconds he said nothing. (I timed it with my DVR and iPhone) Also silent were Keith Hernandez and Ron Darling, his broadcast partners. Whether planned or not, it was masterful broadcasting by three professionals.

As I watched Santana being mobbed by his teammates, I felt as though I was in the stadium. I didn't have some obnoxious loudmouth yelling in my ear. It wasn't about the broadcaster, it was about the moment. Because of the words they *didn't* say, it was a wonderful moment for me, the viewer.

When I called the final out of the Hudson Valley Renegades New York Penn League title in 1999, I tried to employ much the same tactic. After an excited description of the game's final pitch (a strikeout), I let the crowd fill the broadcast air. On radio, I didn't let it go 64 seconds, but surely for 10 or 20 seconds my listeners heard a jubilant crowd and fireworks filling the air. Gary Cohen I'm not, but I'm proud to say I learned a thing or two from Marty Glickman.

How many broadcasters would have let us enjoy that moment by saying nothing?

Reporting in the Dark

Sideline reporting is not easy. At least doing it well is not easy.

Sure, any flashy former player or former cheerleader can talk for thirty seconds, delivering a prepared bit of information. And that's what we usually get - a canned piece of news just as easily delivered by the color analyst.

Occasionally, however, we get to see what real sideline reporting is all about. The ability to bring us something unique, that only a reporter on the sideline could gather.

In my opinion, that is exactly what Steve Tasker and Solomon Wilcots - both former players - were able to do during Super Bowl XLVII in 2013. When the lights went out in the Superdome, these guys were ready.

When the broadcast booth lost power completely, CBS was forced to come back from a commercial to Tasker and Wilcots. It's not an easy task to ad-lib, inform the viewer, and throw it across the field to your colleague. To do so smoothly, in front of the entire country, is not as simple as it looks. It truly isn't. I thought Tasker and Wilcots were stellar and completely up to the moment on a huge stage.

Of course there are those who disagree with my take completely. Chris "Mad Dog" Russo, whom I worked with briefly as an intern at WFAN Radio in NY in 1998, made it very clear that he felt Tasker, Wilcots and the entire CBS crew were caught with their pants down. He wasn't impressed. I was. Especially considering these two guys were professional athletes, rather than career-trained broadcasters.

No, sideline reporting is not easy. Especially while standing in the dark, an entire nation hanging on your every word.

Off the Record

As sports fans, we often think we know what players are thinking. On the field we assume they must be anticipating the next play or contemplating strategy. Off the field, we assume they don't have a worry in the world. Well, we know what happens when we assume....we are often *very* wrong! It turns out that quite regularly the players are focused on *the broadcasters*!

Broadcasters get a candid, eye-opening look into the *real* thoughts going through players' heads during a game. While broadcasting for a professional baseball team in the mid 1990's I had a second baseman say he was always looking up at us in the broadcast booth, wondering what we were talking about. He yearned to switch spots. (I would have obliged) Another time, the third base coach turned toward my broadcast perch above the third base dugout and actually answered a question I had posed to listener on the air.

Perhaps one of the strangest encounters I had was when a player called me aside one day before the game. There was something on his mind.....something that seemed to be causing him some real distress. We had become quite friendly, and he had recently introduced me to his wife.

"Do me a favor," he said. "Please don't mention on the air anything about my wife."

It turns out that the two had married hurriedly without the knowledge of either family. His concern was that I would spill the beans on the air, where his parents and family would hear back home via the streaming internet broadcast. I would blow the whole thing!

Never in a million years did I think this star player would be worried about something I - the lovable broadcaster - would say on the air.

I never once mentioned his secret - until now. But I certainly thought about it often, each time I saw him on television playing in a big league uniform.

Getting Fired

Getting fired is part of the sports broadcasting industry. Sometimes you deserve it, and sometimes you don't. But most sportscasters get fired - axed, let go, laid off, canned - at some point in their career. Sometimes we can turn it into a learning opportunity.

Occasionally, we'll see broadcasters canned when something untoward emerges from their online past. These instances can be teachable moments for all aspiring sportscasters. Everything you do is part of building your reputation and brand. Facebook, YouTube, Twitter and the like are all potential focal points of prospective employers or fans. Use them responsibly, and at your own risk.

Sportscasters must do everything in their power to protect their good name and reputation. Build your sports broadcasting career on a solid moral compass to prevent your career from being needlessly derailed.

Technology is great, however far too often we see sportscasters jeopardizing their careers or alienating their audiences through unwise, provocative use of social media. Take caution, and remember why you have your platform in the first place.

My Sports Broadcasting Nightmare

All sportscasters have dreams. Some yearn to make the big leagues. Others hope to call a Super Bowl on national TV.

I have a sportscasting nightmare.

For 25 years, since I started calling games, I've had a recurring nightmare. Not often, perhaps a couple times a year.

I'm sitting in the broadcast booth and the game is beginning. The pitcher fires one in and the batter smacks it into the outfield. As he whips around the bases, my heart is pounding.
Who is this batter? What is the pitcher's name? And beyond that, where am I and who are these two teams? This is MY sportscasting nightmare - the dreaded fear of being unprepared.

It was this dream that always had me preparing hours before the first pitch. Usually a few hours of prep for each hour of on-air action. And it didn't matter the sport. For Army hoops games, I'd spend time the week prior, during practice, walk-thru's and the day of the game. Professional baseball was a never-ending prep fest.

For year during Sports Broadcasting classes, I've implored students to over-prepare and plan for all contingencies.

As a fan or professional, what is your sports broadcasting nightmare?

Spring Training is a Joke

Let's be honest. Spring Training is a sham.

I mean, it's six weeks of fluff. Virtually meaningless, like drinking decaf coffee in the morning.

Don't get me wrong, counting down the days until pitchers and catchers report is something all baseball fans can truly get behind. The winter thaw is near, the darkest days of the year stretch longer, and somewhere Dave Magadan is hitting fungos. Baseball's yearly emergence is a wonderful thing.

I'm just saying that six weeks for well-paid, highly regimented professional athletes is much more than they need to prepare. After all, with millions riding on each season, players stay in tip-top shape year-round. Many say they take a couple weeks off and are back to it before Thanksgiving.

Years ago, players needed Spring Training to get back into playing shape. Those off-seasons earning a living by working retail, painting houses or digging graves like Ritchie Hebner are long gone. These days, the off-season job is to improve for next season.

Players today are world-class professional athletes. And, barring injuries, managers have their game plan in mind well in advance. The real purpose of Spring Training is to create a mini-season for fans to buy tickets, merchandise, hotel rooms, restaurant meals and to reassert their love for the game.

Spring Training is a terrific time of year. Even if it is a sham.

Tenure

Baseball is known for its colorful characters and hilarious moments. Where fact meets fiction, sometimes it's hard to tell.

Take, for example, one of baseball's best players of all-time.

The story goes that one day, while riding on the team bus to the ballpark, this baseball immortal overheard a couple teammates discussing longevity in the game and retirement.

Ask he inched closer, the young player asked him,

"Hey, you've got tenure, right?"

"Ten years?" The star shot back quickly. "I've got twenty years in the big leagues!"

Care to guess who that was?

The Cheat Goes On

The great Dave Ramsey often says that high-income earners can fall prey to "doing stupid with zeros at the end." In other words, we all make mistakes, but with increased wealth comes the possibility of bigger, more costly mistakes.

I'm reminded of this each time we hear yet another round of Performance Enhancing Drug allegations.

The fact is, baseball players have always cheated. Or should I say, "stretched beyond the written rules to gain an edge." Take this brief list, for example:

- Pine tar

- Amphetamines

- Scuffing

- Stealing signs

- Petroleum Jelly

- Corked bats

- Steroids

- HGH

- Synthetic PEDs

- iWatches

Baseball players have always looked for an advantage, and always will. They were cheating 20 years ago, 10 years ago, 1 year ago, last week and today. They will cheat tomorrow and next season too.

The only difference now is that today, through remarkable innovation, the methods of cheating are beyond anything we've ever seen. We've gone from cork and greenies to synthetics and technology.

I heard all the rumors and stories when broadcasting in the 90's, and some guys I knew well were eventually named in the Mitchell Report.

Players are only human. They're going to cash in when possible. The big difference, today they are cashing in with zeros at the end.

The Most Difficult Sport to Broadcast

"Baseball is the most difficult sport to broadcast. I can't believe how tough it is to call a baseball game!"

I hear that all the time....and I couldn't disagree more.

I usually counter by saying, "Yes, but only if you don't prepare."

My belief is that, with rigorous and thorough preparation, baseball is the easiest and most enjoyable game to broadcast. Specifically on radio, calling a baseball game is roughly 10 percent action and 90 percent fill. No preparation, no fill. No fill and you are done.

For this reason I've always felt I am in complete control over how my baseball broadcast evolves. While I cannot control the action, I can always prepare myself to make the most of the subsequent downtime.

On the other end of the spectrum, hockey, basketball and football present a broadcaster with a much higher percentage of action, compared to down time. Not that I would advise just showing up and mailing it in, but with hockey or basketball you may, on occasion, be able to wing it. Baseball offers no such luxury.

I've always ranked the four major sports, in order of radio broadcasting difficulty, as hockey, basketball, football and baseball. They each require unique broadcasting competencies and skills. No two sports are the same.

How would you rank the most difficult sports to broadcast?

The Fastest Kid on the Block

With the 2013 passing of longtime writer and columnist Stan Isaacs, I was once again reminded of the book that has formed my broadcast philosophy. More than a book, it was a man. And one of Stan Isaacs' lasting legacies is that he helped that man tell his story.

In 1996, sports broadcasting pioneer Marty Glickman told his story with Stan Isaacs in *The Fastest Kid on the Block: The Marty Glickman Story*. More than just a broadcaster's how-to manual, the book recapped - among many other fascinating aspects of his life - how Glickman overcame devastating prejudice at the 1936 Olympics in Berlin, Germany.

The second half of THE FASTEST KID ON THE BLOCK tackles the nuts-and-bolts, ins-and-outs of sports broadcasting. In fact, for all the years I have taught Sports Broadcasting at Marist College and Fordham University, I have required students read this important book. My students need to learn Marty Glickman's story, and how he transitioned from world-class athlete to broadcast pioneer. We have weekly quizzes on Marty's life and traditional broadcast philosophy.

I appreciated Marty Glickman each Tuesday in the mid-90's, when he sat with us for hours, critiquing demo tapes to help us improve. When Marty talked, you listened.

I am proud to say Marty's influence continues to this day, as we carry on his legacy at Fordham's WFUV.

The Mystery of Baseball's Winter Meetings

Each year's Baseball Winter Meetings remind me of the meetings I attended in New Orleans in the mid-90's. For me, and thousands of others, the meetings were an opportunity to get in front of minor league clubs and lobby to become their radio voice.

Along with all the Big League wheeling and dealing, a lot of minor league moving and shaking happens at the meetings.

A few of my memories of that exciting week:

-I flew into town sitting next to an owner of multiple minor league teams, including the Norwich Navigators, for whom I called games five years later.

-Sipping a Hurricane at a Bourbon Street bonfire, I chatted with an executive from a Triple-A International League team. His big pearl to me that night – never send a resume on white paper. "I get hundreds of resumes," he said. "I need a way to weed out half of them right away. The white ones get chucked." I always remembered his advice when I paid a few extra bucks for cream-colored resume paper, and we kept in touch for years.

-One morning at the hotel, a flash conga line formed. One woman stood up from her table and started dancing around the restaurant dining room. Table by table, she garnered more followers, until a line of 20 or more was bopping around as if it were the Fourth of July…..at 7 a.m. (No, my briefcase and I did not join. I was there for business, not pleasure)

-I took part in quite a few interviews with clubs, ranging from the Modesto, CA Athletics and the Williamsport, PA Crosscutters. I recall crowded ballrooms, small interview spaces and little sleep. I eventually turned down the Crosscutters gig to remain with the Hudson Valley Renegades.

While the big stars garner most of the Winter Meeting attention, it can be a great chance for an aspiring sportscaster to make some connections and jump-start a career!

Or you can slug Hurricanes, start bonfires and dance around all day. It's a win either way.

A Memorable Dinner

Minor league broadcasters find some of the most unique ways to amuse themselves during bus rides and road trips. This is one reason I've always referred to the minor leagues as a Traveling Freak-Show Circus.

One of my colleagues used to bring his "Book of Questions" on road trips. We'd sit on the bus and take turns answering questions, such as "Would you rather jump into a pool of snakes or take a bath in a tub of spiders?" Or "Would you run naked through a sell-out baseball stadium if, as a result, you would save ten families from poverty?" We spent many overnight hours answering these nonsensical questions and then debating the answers. Oh, the glamour of professional baseball!

One afternoon on the road, a handful of us were catching a leisurely lunch, waiting for the 3:00 bus to the ballpark. Someone at the table posed the question, "If you could have dinner with one person from history, who would it be?" You can imagine some of the answers. Jesus. Babe Ruth. George Washington.

As we cleaned up and prepared to pay the bill, the team's clubhouse manager (and current TV actor!) offered his reply.

"John Lithgow," he said matter-of-factly.
On that note we paid the bill and headed for the early bus. That's minor league baseball for you.

Plenty of Room for Tidbits

There is one tool that every baseball announcer cannot live without. Without this tool, you would lost on the air. You would have no clue. The game would fly by you and your career would end before it ever got started.

What is this one indispensable tool?

Your scorebook, of course.

Whether it's the back of a napkin, or a top-notch, professional quality scorebook, it is the one tool you absolutely must have. A necessity to help you keep up with the rosters, game history and storylines.

I've used many scorebooks in my day. As a teen I used to keep score of games on TV and radio with the basic book you can buy from any sporting goods store.

My broadcasting life changed one day, however, as my broadcast partner, Bill Rogan, bought me my very first Bob Carpenter scorebook. From that day in the mid-90's, I've never broadcast a baseball game without this book.

I've never met Bob Carpenter, and I don't benefit in any way from this recommendation. It just happens to be the very best scorebook I've ever used. The book's layout is exactly as you would wish, with plenty of room for customization. Large writing areas, ample room to keep you organized during that five-hour, 16-inning affair.

The best part about this book - all kinds of extra room for tidbits. As I always say, tidbits make a broadcast, and in baseball you need a ton of them. Interesting facts, figures, stories and anecdotes that make a ballgame a joy to listen to. Bob Carpenter's scorebook has more than enough room to keep you going. Add in a few hours of pre-game prep and you're all set.

This may not be the best book, but it was for me. Check it out, it may help.

Warner Fusselle

I met Warner Fusselle on August 22, 1994. It was my first season calling minor league baseball for the Hudson Valley Renegades. My broadcast partner, Bill Rogan, and I had to deliver a tape to a "This Week in Baseball" producer in South Hackensack, New Jersey. Fusselle was the longtime host of TWIB, and it was quite a thrill to meet a broadcasting icon that day.

I grew up watching "This Week in Baseball." I looked forward to TWIB's airing before a Mets weekend game even more than the game itself. (The show's theme song is my cell phone ring tone) As we stood talking to Warner Fusselle in his crowded office in New Jersey, I recall thinking "I can't wait to tell my Dad I met Warner Fusselle!" He was extremely gracious and cordial, and we had a nice visit. I had met many sports and broadcasting figures that year, but none compared to meeting the *voice* of "This Week in Baseball," Warner Fusselle.

Five years later, I was the basketball play by play voice of the Army Cadets at West Point. On December 20th, Army played Seton Hall at the Meadowlands Arena in New Jersey. Before the game, I introduced myself to Warner Fusselle, who was calling games for Seton Hall. He remembered me from our brief meeting years earlier. We did a great pregame interview, chatting about college hoops and broadcasting in general. It was great to hear him tell stories in his familiar southern voice.

Classic baseball broadcasters have had the ability to come into our home and, in turn, bring us to the ballpark. Ernie Harwell, Marty Glickman and Red Barber had this talent. So did Warner Fusselle. Whether it was "This Week in Baseball," college hoops or the Brooklyn Cyclones, Fusselle had that warm, friendly sound that made you feel like you were watching the game with a friend.

Sports fans truly had a friend in Warner Fusselle.

Watch Out for the P.C. Police

A sportscaster I know related the following story about the ridiculousness of Political Correctness.....

While calling a college hoops game for the campus radio station, the aspiring broadcast professional made an off-handed joke about the team's star player possibly setting off a metal detector at the airport following the game, due to his mouth full of gold teeth.

Within a week, the broadcaster was called into the station's business offices for a closed-door meeting, where station big wigs expressed their dismay about his "racially charged" comments.

"But I didn't say anything about anyone's race," the young sportscaster explained. "He DOES have a mouth full of gold teeth, and I made the joke about it. But I certainly would never even think about a racial joke. He's a basketball player. His color is irrelevant."

The station's stuffy brain trust simply could not allow this kind of conduct on their air, and the broadcaster was subsequently passed over for a big station promotion. In explaining why he had not been chosen for promotion, he was told that his judgement must be questioned for making such "racist" comments.

Later that semester, the sportscaster went searching for advice from an experienced radio professional at the same institution - a black professor whom he, and all others, liked and respected.

In confidence, he told her exactly what he had said on the air, in complete context.

"I didn't hear you mention anything about race," she answered. "Was there something else I missed?"

"Nope," the broadcaster lamented. "This was the one sentence that they said was racist and insensitive. And furthermore, I know guys from all different races that wear gold teeth!"

"Again, you didn't say anything about race," she concluded. "I don't see how you can take a joke about gold teeth to mean anything racial. You never mentioned race, color or ethnicity. I certainly wouldn't have been offended whatsoever."

The moral of the story? Sports broadcasters have many challenges to overcome. Regardless of your intent, the P.C. Police are always lurking just beyond that radio dial, waiting to pounce. Be ready.

The Salty Sports Broadcaster

They are often quite salty. And quite often they are vengeful, spiteful and childish. No, I'm not referring to politicians. I'm talking about sportscasters.

I recall one particular day many years ago, on the final day of our minor league baseball baseball season. The team was on the road, which meant we had a few hours to kill during the morning before heading over to the ballpark for our broadcast.

We were all ornery, all three of us that piled unenthusiastically out of the car that day, arriving at the crowded local mall. We were tired and didn't particularly like malls. And we *really* didn't like the season coming to an end.

As we weaved through the parking lot, walking toward the mall entrance, one of my salty colleagues commented about how this one flashy sports car was parked across two spots, in a move that would make Larry David cringe. The lot was full, but this guy apparently thought he was super important.

Well, on the final day of the season, one of us just wasn't going to take it. He took a sip from his nearly-untouched extra-large soda and launched the sweet drink, splashing it across the windshield of the car.

"I hate when jerks park like that," he said. As we casually sauntered toward the mall, the dark cola oozed down the windshield and across the shiny hood and doors.

Don't mess with the broadcaster. Especially on the final day of the season.

Spill the Beans

In the minor leagues, a baseball team broadcaster can become almost part of the team. The same age as many of the players, the tendency is for the team's voice to blend in and become one of the guys. As such, a broadcaster can learn a lot about A LOT. Often times too much.

For example - who is doing what after games? Who has an opinion about someone else? Who may be using an illegal substance? Who really doesn't want to be playing baseball in the first place? Which players just got into a fist fight? The stream of information is endless. The predicament, then, is what to do with that information.

One golden rule of broadcasting, which often proves wise, is to keep your focus on the field. As a reporter, give the fans an accurate word picture of everything that takes place between the lines. After all, they tune in to hear the game. You give your listener a great experience and stay far away from that grey line.

If something took place on the bus, in the clubhouse or somewhere other than on the field, it doesn't belong in the broadcast. Certainly you can make exceptions to add some flavor to the broadcast, but those should be the exception rather than the rule. This way you protect yourself from controversy, maintain a player's privacy and still give the listener plenty of tidbits and an accurate portrayal of the team and its season.

Broadcasters know a lot, and sometimes more than they want to know. Defined boundaries help wise broadcasters steer clear of problems and keep the listener focused on the game, between the lines. That is, after all, why the tuned in.

Why We Miss Ernie Harwell

Ernie Harwell was a gem of a man. An accomplished poet, inventor, musician, devoted family man, Christian, mentor…..and yes, a pretty good baseball broadcaster as well. 4 years after he passed away, we miss him today as much as ever.

I covered a lot of ballgames in the mid-90's, as a 20-year-old college broadcaster at WFUV Radio at New York's Fordham University. I'd take the D Train from Fordham Road down to Yankee Stadium, catch a pre-game meal, take in batting practice on the field, watch the game and then collect interviews for use on air. For a college-aged sports fan, there was nothing better.

During one of my first assignments, I sat in the Press Lounge, preparing to eat my breakfast before the Yankees' 1:00 game a few hours later. As I jabbed my fork into my scrambled eggs, a hand tapped my table and a gentle voice asked,
"Would it be okay if I sit and eat with you?" It was Ernie Harwell.

I contained my shock and excitement long enough to invite him to sit and join me.

Over the next half hour he shared a lot – tales, advice, insight and perspective on the sports broadcasting industry. Much like the great Marty Glickman, he seemed intent on learning my story and sharing his willingness to help. We had a great breakfast and he even passed me his phone number, in case I needed a tape critiqued in the future. Did I? You bet I did.

Later that season, while broadcasting in the Tampa Bay Devil Rays farm system, I sent Ernie a tape and asked for his thoughts. Soon thereafter we spoke at length on the phone, and he laid out some concrete, real-world ways I could improve. He ended the call by saying, "Rick, just keep on keeping on!"

Today I counsel young sportscasters, and one main theme I constantly try to drill into their head is to take every opportunity to learn from a successful mentor. Ask for insight and most of the time they will provide it to you.

In a day where much of our sportscasting culture is wrapped up around ego-boosting sound bytes, opinion, catch-phrases and clichés, it's refreshing to think back to a man who was never too big to give back.

We all miss Ernie Harwell much more than we realize.

Milk and Cookies

"You can't play this game on milk & cookies!"

I heard that wisdom from a minor league manager about 20 years ago, when the manager heard about his star player's late-night exploits the night before.

Baseball is full of colorful characters and colorful quotes. One of the all-time greats came from Cubs outfielder Hack Wilson, who in 1930 set baseball's all-time single-season RBI record with 191.

Manager Joe McCarthy had become increasingly irritated by Wilson's late-night debauchery, which was legendary. One morning, he called the slugger into his office and closed the door.

On his desk were two clear drinking glasses – one filled with water, the other with whiskey.
McCarthy dropped a live, squirming worm into the water, and watched it squirm. He dropped the second worm into the whiskey, and it immediately went stiff and died.
McCarthy looked up at Wilson and asked, "So what does that tell you?"

"Well," replied the hung-over slugger, "It means that as long as I keep drinking, I won't catch worms!"

Bonus - Baseball Was Made for Radio

"Baseball is better on radio than television because the pictures are better."

A wise baseball fan made this comment one summer day while listening to his favorite ballclub on the radio, and it proves what many of us already believe – that baseball on the radio is special.

Today, baseball on the radio is something we take for granted. We can turn it on or off, and even take it with us. However, that was not always the case. The masterful artwork we hear each season across the national airwaves is a result of years of evolution and change, which have developed the special marriage between radio and baseball.

On June 19, 1846, the first baseball game was played at the Elysian Fields in Hoboken, New Jersey. The game had evolved from other variations played worldwide, and this was believed to be one of the first organized contests of the new baseball in America. (No, the game wasn't invented by Abner Doubleday in Cooperstown)

On that historical summer afternoon in 1846, the New York Nine demolished Alexander Cartwright's Knickerbockers 23 to 1. However, if you weren't at the game, you had no idea it even took place. Radio wasn't there and, therefore, you weren't there. Radio and baseball didn't officially meet until some 70 years later.

Baseball was first broadcast on radio on August 5, 1921. On that day, Harold Arlin and KDKA Radio broadcast a Pirates home game – an 8-5 win over the Phillies at Forbes Field in Pittsburgh. It was a rough-sounding broadcast, with the transmitter going out from time to time and the microphone levels constantly in flux. Far from the technical extravagance we have in today's broadcasts, it was a start.

Later that same year, also on KDKA, world-renowned sportswriter Grantland Rice did the first play-by-play of a World Series game. Additionally, two other stations, WJZ in Newark and WBZ in Springfield, produced their own versions of the game. They each had a man at the Polo Grounds who, via phone, would relay the results of each pitch back to the station. Back at the two studios, someone else would receive the information and re-create the game for his listeners. The art of baseball re-creations was born.

When re-creating a game, the broadcaster didn't have scorecards or media guides, statistics or color analysts. All they had was the information as it trickled in from the ballpark via the wire. The results would be in simple code, such as "B-1-O," meaning "Ball One Outside." The rest was up to the broadcaster.

"Those re-creations entailed a lot of honest imagination," said broadcasting pioneer Marty Glickman, who recalled one particular re-creation from the early 1940's. On that day Bob Feller no-hit the Yankees, and Glickman was re-creating the game after it was completed. He took the facts and created an entertaining broadcast.

To give listeners a better feel for the action, Marty would simulate the bat hitting the ball by smacking a wood block with a wooden hammer. For example, a loud SMACK would be used for a long hit. A slight tap with the wooden hammer would represent a weakly-hit ball.

Glickman was moving along, building the drama of the game with Feller on the mound, when he accidentally gave the wood a really good WHACK! Marty knew that Feller had dominated the Yanks in throwing that no-hitter, and he had just simulated a real wallop.

"I had to think quickly," he said with a chuckle, "I said it was a long fly ball that just curved foul. That was a close one!"

No tale of baseball re-creations would be complete without including the famous story involving future President Ronald Reagan. Young Reagan was re-creating a game in Des Moines, Iowa, in the 1930's. The game was rolling along and Billy Jurges came up...just as the wire went dead!

Reagan is calling the game, with Jurges at the plate and no wire reports. A couple minutes go by as Reagan is killing time, and then he starts having Jurges foul off pitches. He had no choice because he had absolutely no idea what was happening at the ballpark! Jurges fouls one to the left, one to the right, one into the seats where two kids get in a fight for the ball. Until the wire came back, Reagan deftly embellished details and filled time.

Finally, after seven minutes, the wire came back on and the result of the at bat finally came across. Jurges had popped out on the first pitch.

"I listened to the games and knew they were recreated," says Bob Ahrens, Executive Sports Producer of WFUV Radio in New York, "But the fact that they were re-created didn't give the broadcasts any less credibility."

Also in the 1930's came a couple other big broadcasting developments. One stuck, one didn't. The first, which did withstand the test of time, was the introduction of former athletes into the baseball broadcast booth. (Glickman himself was perhaps the first athlete ever to enter the booth, after a stellar career on both the track and football field.)

Former Cleveland outfielder Jack Graney became the voice of the Cleveland Indians, and thus the first ex-athlete to occupy the baseball broadcast booth.

Perhaps the most *notable* ex-athlete broadcaster in baseball's early days was Dizzy Dean, who stepped behind the mic for the St. Louis Cardinals in 1941. The former pitcher was raw, frank and often grammatically incorrect, such as when he would say a runner "slud" into second base.

"Most of the established ex-athletes are pretty good today," says former Vermont Expos radiocaster George Commo.

The second important development in the 1930's was the growing fear of baseball on the radio. While it was flourishing in some parts of the country, it was looked down on in others, especially in New York. Many team owners were afraid that if people could listen to the game at home they wouldn't come out to the ballpark.

"Some minor league general managers are still frightened of that same thing today," said Denver, Colorado radio legend Bill Rogan, "But you have to look at radio as something that enhances baseball, not something that endangers it. A radio broadcast is a three-hour commercial for your team, and if all the games are not broadcast on radio it is a disservice to the fans of that team."

In 1934, the New York Yankees, Giants and Brooklyn Dodgers were so frightened of fans choosing radio over a trip to the ballpark that they signed a pact to bar their broadcasts from radio in New York until 1938. The capital of western civilization -in fact, the mecca of the baseball world - and an official contract *not* to have baseball on the radio! That is simply difficult to comprehend today.

Just two years later, 13 of baseball's 16 teams had radio –
all except the three New York teams! In 1939, Dodgers
owner Larry MacPhail finally gave in and signed a deal
with WOR Radio. The Yankees and Giants were angered,
but they soon succumbed to the pressure and signed radio
deals as well. Each of baseball's 16 teams now had radio
packages to broadcast their games.

"Baseball on the radio is an all-or-nothing thing," says
former Norwich Navigators broadcaster Mark Leinweaver,
"It is absolutely necessary to have all of your games on
radio, and it may prompt some fans to respond to the
excitement and come out to the ballpark."

Over the years, summer afternoons have been filled with
ballgames featuring broadcasting legends such as Bob
Murphy, Gary Cohen, Jon Miller and Vin Scully. These
announcers were not the first, however. Many of today's
greats follow in the footsteps of yesterday's broadcasting
pioneers, such as, Mel Allen, Ernie Harwell and Bob
Prince. Red Barber

In many ways, the craft of baseball broadcasting is like a
house, only as strong as its foundation. Those who come
later try to build on what has already been formed. Tracing
back, this history of baseball broadcasting can help us
understand why things are as they are today.

"I grew up listening to many announcers, including Phil
Rizzuto and Bob Murphy," said Rogan. "These were guys
who entertained, informed and had a good time. I'm sure
that over the years I've incorporated many of their
attributes into my style. At least I hope I have."

"Ned Martin with the Red Sox was my favorite," says Commo. "He was not your typical announcer because he was natural on the air and knew the right times to get excited."

Both the artist and the art have changed and evolved. Re-creations of games have given way to live play-by-play from the actual site. In addition, the first broadcasts in the 1930's were often done with only one broadcaster. There were no color men or sideline reporters – it was one man and a mic.

Today, at least at the major league level, there are both men and women – engineers, statisticians, play-by-play announcers and color analysts. And with growth in the popularity of baseball on radio has come an increase in expectations.

It has long been assumed that radiocasters on the East Coast are held to a different set of standards than those in the Midwest. From 1921 until today, baseball on the radio in the East has been built on a philosophy of objectivity and balance. Sure, the hometown announcer wants "his" team to win, but only because it's more fun to broadcast for a winner than a loser.

The general consensus is that a broadcaster on the East Coast tends to be more objective and less of a "homer" than those in the Midwest. Take a listen to White Sox games, where the Sox don't come to bat. Rather, "the good guys come to bat." Different styles for different parts of the country.

I think, at least traditionally, a lot has to do with the New York East Coach area being the capital of the world," said Rogan. "New York is, and always has been, a melting pot. There probably are more fans of different teams in New York than anywhere else, predominantly because there is more of everyone in New York."

Conversely, in places like St. Louis or Chicago, the entire area tends to be made up of fans of that one team, so announcers tend to reflect that and become favorable to them.

"I think it varies from team to team," says Commo. "It's not just an East-West thing because there are homers everywhere."

Perhaps baseball's most famous radio call was in 1951 when Bobby Thompson hit the "shot heard round the world" as the New York Giants beat the Brooklyn Dodgers and won the National League pennant. Russ Hodges excitedly yelped, "The Giants win the pennant! The Giants win the pennant!" This was a New York broadcaster mirroring the excitement of his listening audience.

"I want a guy with a good voice that will advertise for our team," said one southern minor league General Manager, who was recently in search of a radio announcer. "We don't want our guy to say anything bad about our team. We want a homer and his job will be to root for us."

On the other side, many still believe in objectivity from the broadcast booth.

"A good broadcaster doesn't give opinions," said Glickman. "He simply lets the listener make up his or her own mind. Your job as a broadcaster is to put the listener right next to you in the seat and let him formulate his own opinions."

"There certainly is a fine line you have to walk between objectivity and representing your team," says Leinweaver. "However, you have to be as objective as possible."

The man who said he enjoyed baseball on the radio more because "the pictures are better" brought up the key aspect of baseball on the radio. When an announcer says, for example, "The ball is slapped down the left field line and bounces into the corner," we can see it. The picture in our mind's eye is whatever we create it to be. The listener is an active participant in the game because he completes his own interpretation of the event. We all "see it" uniquely in our minds. That is the beauty.

Before television, radio was all fans had if they weren't in the ballpark. Many fans only knew their baseball heroes from the descriptions of their exploits on radio broadcasts. Huge fans of Joltin Joe DiMaggio or Stan Musial may have gone years feeling like they knew a lot about their heroes, while never setting eyes on them! The only images of the players they may have had were the ones in their minds, created by the descriptions of broadcast pioneers like Red Barber or Mel Allen.

Even with the option of television, baseball flourishes on radio to this day.

The reason is simple – the pictures *are* better.

Special Offer for Sports Broadcasting Students

As a special thanks for reading this book, please enjoy

HALF OFF OUR ONLINE SPORTS BROADCASTING COURSE

Visit Udemy.com/sportscasting

Use special code BOOKVIP

More Sports Books by Rick Schultz on Amazon.com, iTunes and Audible.com - in Kindle, paperback and audio format:

Untold Tales from the Bush Leagues: A Behind the Scenes Look Into Minor League Baseball, From the Broadcasters Who Called the Action
More than 20 minor league baseball broadcasters share the most amazing, unbelievable and hilarious stories they have seen in the minor leagues. You will not believe what goes on in minor league baseball!

A Renegade Championship Summer: A Broadcaster's View of a Magical Minor League Baseball Season
Come along for the ride with the 1999 New York-Penn League Champion Hudson Valley Renegades. Hear from the players and coaches who made it happen, including superstar Josh Hamilton and many other household names! You'll get the true feel of minor league baseball, going behind the scenes with umpires, front office executives, scouts, former players and many more!

Minor League Baseball Revealed: A Secret Tour Inside Our National Pastime
Both books together in this compilation!

Thank you for reading!

CPSIA information can be obtained
at www.ICGtesting.com
Printed in the USA
LVHW100010130123
737039LV00004B/407

9 781973 166016